Tassili's Raw Reality Cafe'

Presents

Raw Recipes on the Go ^{TM}

ISBN-13: 978-1479395286

ISBN-10: 1479395285

ISBN: 978-1-63944-243-0

Author Photographs by Richard Shabazz & Diane Richie

Food Photographs by JimiFigz

Book Production and Design by Jennifer Bliss & Ananda Lo

Book Cover & Formatting by Michael Q. Yates Jr

Original Editing by Jennifer Bliss, Ananda Lo & Tassili Maat

2nd Edition Editing by Stephanie Leona

3rd Edition Editing by Studio Steffanie Productions

Dedication

Special thanks to the Most High, our collective Ancestors, and my personal Ancestors. Thank you to my family and extended family that consists of friends and Raw Reality Staff who without their love, dedication, perseverance, tenacity, and a lile bit of insanity none of this would be possible. To my customers and the countless people who continue to support in a myriad of ways I give continued thanks. Again, without their collective energy the Raw Reality Movement toward optimal health would not be possible.

Asé
Aho

Amen

Namasté

Foreword

The raw revolution is in full swing and showing no signs of slowing down. The world is undergoing major paradigm shifts in all areas, and health is one of them. We see it evidenced in the demand sales and inquiries every day at Sevananda. Through our daily business activities, we have the pleasure and honor of working with some very talented and creative chefs. Atlanta is full of them. We are thought leaders, a community resource, a place of fellowship, a melting pot of faces from all walks of life, and a place where people can be inspired and empowered to live a healthy life. We encourage self-education and taking back your own power by designing your own path of healing with a customized method just for you.

People, like Tassili, simply want to share their passion and gifts with the world, while educating.

Meatless Mondays was a great success and laid the foundation for food demos like In-The-Raw Wednesdays hosted by raw food chef, Tassili Maat. Interest in the living foods lifestyle is on the rise and Tassili has certainly played a significant role in responding with the education necessary to practice it. She was at it long before it became the popular thing to do. Her experience goes way back and continues today at the Raw Reality Restaurant and the I AM Ascension Temple.

I've sampled many of her creations. Curried Plantains, Tofu Delight and Sesame Seaweed Salad are three of my personal favorites. Raw talent, authenticity and pure love are infused into each project, each expansion of who she is and, of course, every recipe. We have living proof and now you do too, inside the pages of Raw Recipes on the Go.

Raw Recipes on the Go is the natural next step in Tassili's continuous evolution and we're excited to be part of it. Inspired by the delectable recipes sampled at In-the-Raw Wednesdays, this un-cook book is a special treat, one you can literally savor. Enjoy!

Ahzjah Netjer Simons

Formerly Sevananda Marketing and Outreach Manager

Currently President of Conscious Living OmniMedia Group

& Founder of The Children's Wellness Network

Introduction

Greetings and kudos to you for loving you and yours enough to choose life! Living foods that are prepared in a loving and efficient manner are essential ingredients for a long and prosperous life. You are what you eat. It's just that simple. What else can the body and mind work with but what you give them? No matter if you are a 100% raw foodist or a meat eater you can benefit from these healthy, delicious and expeditious recipes. You are encouraged to be empowered to explore your own creativity with these recipes as my measurements are all approximations. In other words, if you want to learn to prepare your food the "Tassili's Raw RealityTM" way, you've got to go within and prepare the food in the spirit. Connect with your heart, connect with your food. Don't be timid, dig in! Explore, experiment, massage, rub and roll your food. Taste, see, smell and feel your passion. The way you prepare your food is a direct extension of yourself. Put your highest essence and intentions into your food and it comes back to you. What a blessing that you love yourself that much!

One of main reasons I resisted becoming a raw foodist was that "I just did not have the time to go through all that preparation just to eat"! As the mother of five children and the ex- wife of two "wasbands" (ex-husbands), I found myself doing a lot of single parenting. I was self-employed and still had the two younger children who were teenagers, when I had to make the paradigm shift. In 2008, I had begun having some health challenges which were not only untimely but seemed impossible! I'd been a vegan vegetarian since 1988! Why was I experiencing the onset of arthritis in my fingers? Well after talking with a friend who happened to be an M.D. and a raw foodist, he said I was eating too much starch...gasp!!! I had become a "starchatarian"!!!

So I decided to make a shift. Once I made the commitment to being a 98% raw foodist, after only a year, my paradigm changed easily and forever! That's because I realized that I was already buying fresh foods. I was already

preparing them too. The difference was that now I was prepping to marinate, instead of prepping to sauté, fry or bake! WOW...who knew? And the revelation being that the food was ready to eat a whole lot faster most of the time. So not only was it quick for a mom/entrepreneur on the go, but we were geing the maximum amount of nutrition as well. It was a great supplement for my children too. They were not interested in being raw foodists, but they did enjoy eating it along with the rest of their teenage vegetarian diet.

Realistically I was a "budgetarian" first. I was not always able to buy organic but I did when I could. When I couldn't I would wash the veggies in a lile vinegar and water (1-part vinegar & 3-part water). I used acidic water when available or some of the convenient veggie washes on the market. I always use spring water or alkaline water to soak my food.

The costs were about the same. Let's face it, it's expensive to be healthy in America. You're going to pay for it on the front end or the back. So why not invest in yourself and your family by buying the best you can afford rather than paying on the back end with high medical bills, high insurance and poor health. Learning to shop wisely by simply asking questions, doing some research and experimentation helped. Lile tips can make a big difference!

Thus, Tassili's Raw Reality's Raw Recipes on the GoTM Quick and Easy Raw Food in 15 minutes or Less! Well you're on your way! Be empowered, enjoy, and remember to tap into your own creativity while trying these simple & delicious recipes! The sky's the limit!

Choose life!
Tassili Maat ~ Owner/Chef

Table of Contents

Dedication.. 1

Foreword 2

Introduction 5

The Raw Kitchen 11

Recipes:

Curry Plantains^{TM}................................... 13

Tofu Delight^{TM}.. 15

Zucchini Not Dog^{TM}............................... 16

Rainbow Couscous^{TM}........................... 19

Eggplant Pizza^{TM}................................... 21

Mellow Portobello Mushroom^{TM}.......... 24

Sesame Seaweed Salad^{TM}.................. 26

Wakame Seaweed Salad^{TM}............... 28

Raw Stirred Unfry^{TM}.............................. 29

Seaguac & Sprout Roll^{TM}.................... 31

Green Goddess Guacamole^{TM}........ 33

Hot Salsa^{TM}.. 35

Super Snack^{TM}..................................... 36

Banana Coconut Cream Pie^{TM}........... 37

Pecan Cookies^{TM}... 41

Raw Chocolate Delights^{TM}..................... 43

Testimonies.. 46

Fun Facts.. 49

The Raw Kitchen

The following basic kitchen equipment is all that's needed for the recipes in this book:

- Blender (one with high rpm & power is best)

- Food Processor

- Coffee Grinder (or Vitamix)

- Knives, Strainer, Grater, etc.

Here are some optional items that will help with raw food preparation and broaden your capabilities:

- Juicer – Mostly makes fresh veggie juice, but brands like "Champion" also make nut butters, pates, etc.

- Vitamix – Blender that makes smooth smoothies, warm soups, flours, nut butters and much more.
- Saladacco—Makes thin veggie noodles.
- Dehydrator—Dehydrates any-thing, and with the temperature set below 110°, food will stay living and re-tain their enzymes. A dehydrator opens up a whole new world of live food options.

It just takes a little more initiative.

** Please remember Tassili's recipes are not exact measurements. You can vary a little more of this and a little less of that, even mix and match ingredients ac-cording to your taste. These measure-ments are given for basic guidance ~ Tassili encourages your creativity!!

Curry Plantains™

INGREDIENTS

3 Plantains
1/2 Red Bell Pepper
1/2 Green Bell Pepper
1/4 Red Onion
1/2 cup of Agave
Pinch of Salt to Taste
2 tablespoons Mild Curry
2 to 3 pinches of Cayenne (Optional)

PREPARATION

Peel plantain and cut into bite size cubes

Cut bell peppers into smaller bite size cubes

Cut onion into smaller bite size cubes

Put in a bowl

Mix by hand

Add curry

Add agave

Gently massage

Salt or 2-3 pinches of cayenne can be added to taste (Optional)

Add LOVE and they're ready!!

Tofu Delight ™

INGREDIENTS

1 1⁄4 oz. container of firm organic Tofu
1⁄4 to 1⁄2 cup of Nutritional Yeast
1⁄4 to 1⁄2 cup Extra Virgin Olive Oil
Cubed Red Onion

1⁄4 cup sliced Black Olives
Sundried Tomatoes julienned (thin strips)
3⁄4 teaspoon of Spike (Spike seasoning available at Sevananda) Optional: Salt to taste

PREPARATION

Crumble tofu in a bowl with your hands
Add nutritional yeast, Spike, and olive oil
Add remaining ingredients
Massage firmly, lovingly into an egg salad like consistency

Add LOVE and it's ready!!

Zucchini Not Dog^{TM}

INGREDIENTS

3 Zucchinis
2 medium Carrots
10 Garlic Cloves
1/3 bag of Kelp Noodles
1⁄2 tablespoon of Extra Virgin Olive Oil 1 tablespoon of Spike (Season to taste) 3-4 slices of Olives (Garnish)
Saran Wrap

16

SAUCE INGREDIENTS

4 tablespoons of Vegenaise
4 tablespoons of Nutritional Yeast Juice
of 2 Lemons

PREPARATION

Cut zucchini in half & scoop out center
with 1/2 teaspoon size scoop.
Take the zucchini center and place in a
food processor.
Add carrots, garlic, kelp noodles, olive
oil and spike to taste and blend.
Put the saran wrap over the zucchini
bed and dip out the Not DogTM filling
and fill up the zucchini bed.

Turn zucchini on its side so that you are
rolling the Not DogTM mixture into the
plastic. Twist the ends in opposite direc-
tions.
Not DogTM can be served right away,
however refrigerating for an hour gives
a firmer finish.

This recipe makes six Not Dogs TM

SAUCE PREPARATION

Mix veganaise, nutritional yeast and lemon juice together and spread on Not DogTM. Add sliced olives for garnish (Optional)
Add LOVE and it's ready!

Rainbow Couscous™

INGREDIENTS

2 cups of Couscous
1 cup of:
*Mulberries
*Black & Yellow Raisins *Dried Papaya
Any combination of dried fruits i.e.,
Pineapples, Dates, etc. Salt
Extra Virgin Olive Oil

PREPARATION

Place 2 cups of couscous in a bowl
Cover couscous with water:
Add water up to 1 inch above the couscous & set aside to soak (the water will rehydrate couscous)
While couscous is soaking: Cut the dried papaya into cubes Add cubed papaya to bowl of couscous
Add mulberries & raisins
Add 2 pinches of salt

Add 3 tablespoons of extra virgin olive oil
Place all items in the bowl and mix together with your hands (Note: Gently mix to keep couscous fluffy)
Add LOVE and it's ready!!

Eggplant Pizza ™

INGREDIENTS

2 medium sized or 1 large Eggplant 1 1/2
to 2 cups of Sundried Tomatoes 7 fresh
Garlic Pearls
Basil
Thyme
Oregano
Marjoram
Parsley
14 Black Pitted Olives
1 cup Nutritional Yeast (may vary w/ size
of pizza) 1 Red, Yellow, and Green Pepper
1 Red Onion
Garlic Powder (optional)

PREPARATION

Slice eggplant(s) into 1-inch thick circles
Perforate both sides of eggplant with a fork
Massage olive oil into eggplant
Massage garlic powder into eggplant (optional)
If sundried tomatoes have not been hydrated, place in water for 45 minutes to an hour

If sundried tomatoes have been hydrated (or there is no time to hydrate) place them into the food processor and gradually add water to become a paste
Halfway before becoming a paste, add fresh herbs and garlic pearls
Take three stalks of each herb, strip the leaves

Place leaves into food processor
Add a quarter to half cup of olive oil to get desired thickness
While paste is sitting, slice olives into three parts
Cube or mince onions and bell peppers

Spread paste/sauce on top of eggplant a quarter inch thick, like you're spreading pizza sauce

Mix onions, olives, peppers, and sprinkle on top

Sprinkle nutritional yeast on top

Add LOVE and it's ready!!

MELLOW PORTOBELLOW MUSHROOM

<u>INGREDIENTS</u>

1 to 2 Avocados
1/2 Cup Arame Seaweed
1 Portobello Mushroom
1/4 teaspoon of Trocomare' (Seasoning available at Sevananda) 7 Cherry Tomatoes
1 healthy pinch of Sprouts
1/4 cup of Extra Virgin Olive Oil
A sprinkle of Hemp Seeds
1 teaspoon of Garlic Powder
Optional: Cayenne Pepper

PREPARATION

Soak Arame in water to rehydrate
Take off the stem of the mushroom
Take Portobello and perforate with a knife
Massage olive oil into mushroom
Sprinkle garlic powder on mushroom then massage into mushroom
Mash avocado with hands in a bowl
Add Trocomare' and rehydrated Arame and mix all together with hands Place avocado on the Portobello bed
Cut tomatoes and stem into cubes and place in the center of guacamole Place sprouts on the top and place half cherry tomatoes in center of sprouts Sprinkle hemp hearts & add cayenne pepper (optional)
Add LOVE and it's ready!!

Sesame Seaweed Salad^{TM}

INGREDIENTS

Arame Seaweed Raw Sesame Seeds
Toasted Sesame Oil Mineral Salt
1 bunch Scallions

PREPARATION

Take the Arame seaweed and place in a bowl (1 cup per individual serving) Add water 1 inch above the seaweed (The water will rehydrate the seaweed) While seaweed is soaking, chop scallions After soaking for 10 minutes, drain off excess water

Add 1 tablespoon of raw sesame seeds
Add a pinch of salt
1/4 to 1/2 cup of toasted sesame oil
Place all items in the bowl and mix together with your hands

Add LOVE and it's ready!!

WAKAME SEAWEED SALAD ™

INGREDIENTS

Wakame Seaweed
1 Cucumber
1 Sweet Yellow Pepper 1 Sweet Red Pepper
1 Sweet Orange Pepper 3-4 Lemons

PREPARATION

Take the Wakame seaweed and place in a bowl
(1 cup per individual serving)
Add water 1 inch above the seaweed & set aside to soak (the water will rehydrate seaweed)

While seaweed is soaking:
Peel and cube 1 whole cucumber Cube each pepper
Squeeze the juice of 3 to 4 lemons

Pour the excess water off the seaweed
Place all items in the bowl and mix together with your hands

Add LOVE and it's ready!!

Raw Stirred Unfry™

INGREDIENTS

1 package of Kelp Noodles
Gluten Free Tamari (to taste)
1/2 cup of shredded Carrots
1 tablespoon Hemp Hearts
1/2 cup of Shredded Zucchini
1 tablespoon of Chia seeds
1/2 cup of Purple Cabbage
Sprinkle of fresh ginger
1/2 cup of Yellow Squash
2 tablespoons of Extra Virgin Olive Oil

½ cup of Chard or Bok Choy
½ cup of Snap Peas
½ cup of Broccoli
1 package of Sprouts

PREPARATION

Take noodles out & cut them in half or in thirds
(depending on how long you want noodles to be)
Place all items in the bowl and mix together with your hands

Add LOVE and it's ready!!

SEAGUAC & SPROUT ROLL™

INGREDIENTS

2 to 3 Avocados
1 stalk of Scallion
3⁄4 to 1 teaspoon Spike (to taste)
1 Lemon (juiced)
1 oz. Seaweed ~ Either Wakame, Hijiki or Arame 4 to 5 Sheets of Nori
1/3 cup chopped Tomatoes
1⁄2 container of Sprouts (Alfalfa or Mung Bean)

PREPARATION

**SEAGUAC
Soak seaweed approximately 10 minutes
Mash avocados into creamy texture
Cut scallion into small pieces
Add Spike & lemon juice
Drain excess water off seaweed & add to mixture Mix lovingly with your hands

** NORI ROLL
Lay out Nori Sheets and add a line of Seaguac

Add chopped tomatoes and a thin layer
of sprouts
Roll up tightly and seal with water on
the last inch of Nori Sheet

Add LOVE and they're ready!!

GREEN GODDESS GUACAMOLE™

INGREDIENTS

1 Avocado, mashed by hand. ~ Do not use food processor 2 Scallions (or 1/4 onion)
1/4 Tomato
Cayenne

Salt or Spike (contains nutritional yeast) or other flavorings Fresh Garlic
Optional Ingredients
Cilantro, Cucumber, Salsa, Lemon or Lime

PREPARATION

Mix all by hand ~ should be somewhat chunky

Add LOVE and it's ready!!

S<small>ALSA</small> – H<small>OT</small> & S<small>weet</small>^{TM}

INGREDIENTS

4 Roma Tomatoes Hot Peppers

5 Scotch Bonnet 5 Finger Peppers chili peppers

1 Bulb Garlic
A little Spring Water
1⁄2 lemon or lime flesh ~ de-seeded

A few Medjool dates ~ de-seeded
Cilantro

PREPARATION

Blend until smooth

Add LOVE and it's ready!!

Super Snack ™

INGREDIENTS

2 cups of Flax Mill
1 cup of Hemp Hearts
1 cup Almond Powder
1 oz. of Spirulina
1 cup of Goji Berries
1 lb. of Dates
1 cup of Raisins
1 oz. Chia Seeds
Coconut Flakes (optional)

PREPARATION

Put all items in a food processor with 1/2 cup to 1 cup of water and blend until a paste consistency is reached
Take it out of food processor and knead it with flax
Blend almond powder & coconut flakes (optional)

Roll into balls with the almond powder

Add LOVE and they're ready!!

BANANA COCONUT CREAM PIE ™

INGREDIENTS

2 cups of Whole Almonds
1 1/2 cups of Flax Mill
1 cup of Pitted Dates
6 Bananas (3 for pie filling, 3 for slicing)
7oz. Coconut Flakes (For pie filling &
garnish) 1/2to3/4cupAgave

PREPARATION

CRUST:

- Place 2 cups of almonds ina food processor & blend with flax mill (this makes almond flour)

- Mix the almond flour with just enough water in the food processor & add the dates to make a slight paste

- Knead by hand. When it hasfirm shape, put it in a pie plate and mold out into a crust (Lightly sprinkle additional flax mill on pie plate to keep from stick-ing & easily remove pie)

FILLING:

- Mix 3 bananas, coconut flakes and agave in a food processor (add agave slowly to achieve a custard con-sistency)

- Slice 3 bananas (no more than 1/2inch thick each) and fill up pie plate with 2 layers of bananas

- Take the filling and pour in the pie plate, spread it evenly in the pie crust (use a spatula), so that everything is evenly distributed

- Take remaining coconut flakes and sprinkle over the top, completely covering the pie

- Take 5 slices of bananas and arrange in a flower in center

(One in the center & the remaining into a flower design)

  • Take a wedge of fresh lemon, squeeze on to finger, and apply to-bananas on the top of pie (to stop them from oxidizing & keep the color)
Add LOVE and they're ready!!

(Refrigerate for a minimum of 2 hours for firmer texture)

PECAN COOKIES ™

INGREDIENTS

2 cups of Whole Pecans

1 1/2 cup of Flax Mill
1 cup of Pitted Dates

1/2 to 3/4 tablespoons Apple Pie Spice

1 cup of Chopped Pecans

PREPARATION

Blend 2 cups of whole pecans in a food processor with flax mill (This will make pecan flour)
Then put dates in the food processor with just enough water to make a slight paste

Place ingredients in a bowl and add chopped pecans
Blend it up by hand
Sprinkle additional flax mill and knead into a dough consistency (like play-dough)
Roll out on a cutting board and cut out each cookie

Either eat as soft dough cookies or de-hydrate them
for 12 to 16 hours
Add LOVE and they're ready!!

RAW CHOCOLATE DELIGHTS™

INGREDIENTS

1 cup Raw Organic Cacao

(1 cup for every 20 strawberries)

1 cup of organic: *Strawberries *Sliced Apples *Nuts

*Dried Fruit

~ Use any combination or all of the above ~

Pinch of Salt to Taste

Coconut Flakes Optional Cayenne Optional

You can substitute Carob for Chocolate
Optional Sweetener Substitutes:
Date Powder or Paste
Maple Syrup

1⁄2 to 3⁄4 cup of Agave

PREPARATION

Mix cacao & agave in a bowl by hand and dip delectables (strawberries, etc.) Lay on serving tray or a nice plate and serve
You can also serve as candy
When serving as candy, freeze delectables for 3 to 4 hours

(this makes them firm)
For an added touch arrange delectables in a pattern and dribble cacao in design on plate or tray

Add LOVE and they're ready!!

TESTIMONIES

"A long time ago, I was introduced to an Ital Livity through Rastafari, and have been a vegetarian for quite a few years. The next step was to be vegan. Now RAW VEGAN! I have always incorporated raw foods into my Ital Livity. Blessed because of my work here at Sevananda, it is easy to be vegan. And because of Tassili and her un-cooking classes at the I Am Ascension Temple and her demos at Sevananda I learned to prepare many raw dishes. It is easy and fun and a lifestyle that has made me maintain a healthy and youthful temple. When I eat food prepared by Tassili Maat it makes me joyful. Her food is soooooo yummy!! And beautiful and healthy!! I don't like regular seaweed (only Nori) but her Sesame Seaweed dish is something I have grown to love, it's just that good! I encouraged Tassili to become a part of the Sevananda family through outreach demos and in-store demos. I am quite proud of that fact and love to hear her teach our customers how to prepare raw food dishes that jump off the table. She is quite informative and very personable. Tassili is a wonderful example of a person striving to help the community through her passion."

 Ifini Sheppard
Marketing & Outreach Assistant
Sevananda Natural Foods Market

"I have never been fascinated with Raw food beyond salads, but when Tassili started doing In-The-Raw-Wednesdays at Sevananda, she would always make sure I tried whatever she was preparing at the time and it has really changed my view on Raw Foods...her Green Goddess Guacamole wraps are absolute heaven!"

Tasha Tavaras
Former General Merchandise Buyer/ Arts and Education Coordinator Sevananda Natural Foods Market

"I have been eating raw food since 2006, and I have to admit that it can be a less than tasty experience, but Tassili Maat 'puts her foot in it'! Where I come from (Mississippi) that is a huge compliment to the Chef. Her food is artistic, tasty, and it heals the body. A rare raw reality! Thank you Tassili."

 Carolyn Renée Khemra Ast

Human Resources Director Sevananda Natural Foods Market

Fun Facts:

80% of your "diet" should be a "live-it" consisting of raw foods and Tassili's Raw

Reality caters raw food for parties, events, weddings, meetings, etc. Raw foods can be seasoned, marinated and totally delicious!

Marta Bus #71 takes you down Ralph David Abernathy Blvd., and can drop you off right at Tassili's Raw Reality.

Tassili's Raw Reality Wraps are now sold at vegan/vegetarian Co-Op Sevananda Natural Foods Market in Little Five Points ~ the fun part of town? And they have a hot bar, an organic salad bar, groceries, bulk herbs & other bulk food & Wi-Fi.

Kale is high in Vitamin K, which helps to protect against various cancers. Nutritional yeast is high in B vitamins, especially niacin.

Yoga is a great form of strength training. And there are yoga classes upstairs.

Preparing raw foods is easy. You don't even need a stove and Tassili teaches a variety of raw food "un-cooking" classes. **Look for class schedules on**

www.TassilisRawReality.com

Tassili's Raw Reality has events and gatherings. Our biggest event is the highly anticipated Annual Wonderful Wizards of Raw ~ A Raw Foods Extravaganza.
Look for our events on

www.TassilisRawReality.com

The **I AM Ascension Temple of Love** (upstairs) provides rooms that can be rented for study groups, parties, meetings, classes and other functions.
Look for our events on

www.IamAtempleOfLove.com

Supporting small businesses is vital for sustaining a community.

There is ancient wisdom waiting to be remembered by you, and we look forward to seeing you.

Atlanta's Raw Vegan Café

Food for the Body, Mind, Soul & Spirit

1059 Ralph Abernathy Boulevard SW

Atlanta, GA 30310

In the Historic West End Atlanta

DINE-IN | TAKE-OUT | CATERING |Wi-Fi
Phone: 404.343.6126
Open Monday-Sunday 11am-9pm

www.TasilisRawReality.com

Made in the USA
Columbia, SC
22 December 2024

50526126R00035